The Timing *of* Everything PROMISED

Faith Journey Publishing

The Timing of Everything PROMISED
Copyright 2023 by Faith Journey Publishing

Published 2023
Printed in the United States of America
ISBN: 979-8-9858168-4-6

Compiled and edited by Mari Fitz-Wynn
Publications Coordinator: Kimball Honoré McNeal
Illustrator by Nicki Black
Cover design by Leah Morrison

For information, contact:
Faith Journey Publishing, LLC
contact@faithjourneypublishing.com

Contents

FOREWORD

I grew up in church. One of the first photographs I have of my parents and me, after we emigrated to the U.S., is of the three of us in front of a church. I was eight months old. God's promises were whispered to me in Korean.

It has been years since I regularly attended church. I was decolonizing my faith before the process of untangling my faith from Western cultural norms had a label, but I am still a Christian, a believer, a follower of Jesus. I still hear and sit with God's promises, albeit while also asking a lot more questions for God. I am starting to feel like it might be time to step back into a church building, but the desire has nothing to do with programming, the quality of musical worship, or even the charisma of the preacher.

It is to be with other people who believe in, have heard and spoken of, and hope for the ridiculous promises of God, especially when I am tired or hopeless. Just this week, my mom, who is in her mid-70s, and dad, who is in his early 80s, attended Holy Week sunrise prayer services at church, and they reminded me they prayed for my family and me. That is what being in a family of faith is like—someone somewhere is always praying for you, praying with you, even when you cannot find the words let alone the energy to get up before the sun.

The authors of *The Timing of Everything PROMISED* are part of my family of faith. I only know one of the authors, but in their words, I found myself sitting with sisters generous with their honesty and unflinching testimony of faith. They whisper and boldly proclaim God's promises without ignoring disappointment and heartache and without overplaying joy and healing.

Pull up a chair with a blanket and your beverage of choice. Soak in their words and take your time with their wise stories. You may find yourself recalling promises you thought you or God had forgotten.

~Kathy Khang, author of *Raise Your Voice* and co-author of *Loving Disagreement*.

Introduction

Has God ever fulfilled a promise in your life? Have you ever experienced the joy of a promise fulfilled by God? No matter how your present circumstances look, there is a promise in the Word of God for your particular situation. No matter what we face, God's promises will always outweigh what may seem hopeless or unattainable.

God does much of His work in secret. According to His divine plan for our individual lives, He will often work in others who are part of our story to fulfill His promises.

Many theologians agree there are over 8,000 promises written in the Bible, and the wonderfully staggering reality is that we can daily count and see the myriad of God's promises fulfilled in our lives. That possibility should excite you! It certainly does me.

Eight women have lent their voices to this work. Throughout this book, God's promises to heal, provide, restore, comfort, rescue, protect, call, encourage, and love us are written into each story. In many ways, each writer's life story mirrors those of the women from the pages of the Old and New Testament.

Rahab, whose lifestyle had plunged her to the lowest depth of society, was part of God's plan to bring His people to victory. There's Naomi, widowed, sorrowful, and uncertain of her future, yet not alone because of the love of a God who provided for her through the faithful loyalty of her daughter-in-law. Deborah, the Judge, was called to serve in a capacity that had for ages been reserved for men only. Still, her fearless response to step in gave yet another victory for Israel. Esther was equally brave in her own right, standing strong in the face of personal losses, hard questions, and threats for her people. Mary learned to be content to rest and be taught by Jesus rather than letting daily distractions lure her away. Finally, there's Lydia, the businesswoman who came to understand how to bless the church and ministry of Paul with her finances. Like the women throughout the Bible and the women who have contributed to this anthology, all of them have at one time or another desired—needed—the impossible and improbable to happen in their lives. Each may have wept, wailed, or wondered about their situations. Yet, they all patiently waited because they desired or needed the fulfillment of a promise. Most importantly, they knew and trusted the Promise Keeper. And, according to Ephesians 2:4a "God who is rich in mercy..." did not allow it to be otherwise.

We are all on a journey, and the longer we've lived, the farther back we can see and appreciate how faithful God has been. We are promised an abundant life; however, it does not preclude pain, suffering, heartache, and loss.

"I have told you these things so that in Me you may have peace. You will have suffering in this world. Be courageous! I have conquered the world" (John 16:33 HCSB).

Sometimes the promise is delayed through no fault of our own but because of the actions of others. Finding patience and joy in the waiting is the challenge, but holding firmly to the promise will keep our eyes and our affection on the Lord. After being estranged from his family for decades, when they finally were reconciled, Joseph assured them that when they sold him as a young man to a passing caravan, their intent was evil, but God had turned it into good so their lives and the lives of their families would be preserved—a forty-year wait for the fulfillment of a promise shown in a dream.

God's promise to never leave our side, to hold us securely in the palm of His hand, gives us the courage to go on. We never need to settle into discouragement, dismay, or defeat, for His promises are innumerable, as are the new mercies He gives us every morning. (Lamentations 3:22-23). God's promises override every challenge presented in this life, and we have access to Him, and each promise, every day.

"Blessed be the Lord, Who daily loads us with benefits, The God of our salvation! Selah." (Psalms 68:19 NKJV).

I am convinced that what helps—what is our only hope and joy—is knowing, believing, leaning on, and walking in the multitudinous promises of God. When God fulfills a promise, it feels like a special occasion—a sweet celebration for the soul.

"He will once again fill your mouth with laughter and your lips with shouts of joy," (Job 8:21 NLT).

Letting God Be Enough

"…And they lived happily ever after."

My heart glowed as plot twists and turns eventually led the characters in *Seven Brides for Seven Brothers* and *Cinderella* to find their one true love, I thrived on heart-wrenching movies like *A Warm December* and *Love Story*. As a moody, hormonal teenager, I cried copious tears when the characters found romance but lost it to a cruel disease, an accident, or some other disaster. I didn't care as long as my heart broke. These tragic love stories never overshadowed my deep belief in a happy ending in all things for myself.

When I went away to college, the Christian landscape on my campus was different from anything I had ever experienced. I was a church girl from a denomination with a stringent dress code, who only wore dresses with a slip and pantyhose to church—even in summer. No flashy jewelry or makeup was encouraged. At the new church in my college town, I was free to wear jeans, a face full of makeup, and earrings that swept my shoulders—things I would never wear to church back home where my grandfather was the pastor. At Bible studies and discussion groups on campus, I was taught God was more interested in my interior life than my external style, and since it was cool with God, I was going to be cute for Jesus. I became a walking explosion of hot pink, acid green, striped headbands, eight bracelets, and oversized shoulder pads—trying to be a PG version of Cindy Lauper or Whitney Houston.

While I was in college, I was drawn to the emergence of exciting teaching in churches and certain ministries. Its core tenets included how God wants you to have all the desires of your heart; all you had to do was name it—tell God what you wanted and claim it—and speak your desire out loud every chance you got. Another wildly popular teaching I ascribed to taught Jesus suffered in His earthly life so His followers would not have to. It made complete sense that God would show His love for His children by giving us everything we wanted. *Here's the way to my happily ever after.*

The downside of this new gospel taught that if you didn't get what you desired, either your faith was too small, or you were harboring a secret sin that God didn't like. Still, I embraced everything about these teachings, and the people who taught them-were my rock stars.

I jumped right into a new journaling craze and excitedly bullet-listed what I wanted. The list helped me to name it so I could claim it.

- A husband who adored me

- Four children—two girls and two boys

- A world-wide worship music ministry

- Annual first-class trips around the world

- A new vehicle every two or three years

- A grand piano and in-home studio

By no means is this list complete. I also wrote down verses in my journal that I thought supported my desires.

"Delight yourself in the Lord, and He will give you the desires of your heart" (Psalms 37:4 AMP).

"For I know the plans that I have for you,' declares the Lord, 'plans for prosperity and not for disaster, to give you a future and a hope" (Jeremiah 29:11 NASB).

Any verses that challenged my happily–ever-after view were pushed aside, despite the gentle prompting on the inside. For example, "God is our refuge and strength, a very ready help in time of trouble" (Psalms 46:1 NASB). I didn't focus on in time of trouble, just the refuge, help and strength part.

"I have suffered the loss of all things, and count them mere rubbish, so that I may gain Christ...that I may know Him and the power of His resurrection and the fellowship of His sufferings..." (Philippians 3:8, 10 ESV).

Uh-oh...that verse can't be right, either. These verses seemed to indicate the Apostle Paul welcomed suffering. I was conflicted but ignored the disconnect between what I believed and what was in the written text.

A few years after college, I married my husband, and we decided to establish our careers before having children.

I didn't know I was pregnant when I had my first miscarriage. The pain was excruciating, and I knew it wasn't my regular monthly cramps. I was at work but could drive myself to my gynecologist's office before the huge surge of blood flowed.

Three years later, with a new job offer for my husband and a move from Pennsylvania to North Carolina, I was pregnant again, and ready to become a family of three, instead of a couple as we had been for twelve years. I'd reached thirteen weeks and bought a copy of *What to Expect When You're Expecting*. I felt like I could exhale and enjoy the next few months. My parents were excited about their first grandchild.

We'd been in North Carolina for less than seventy-two hours when the familiar cramping and spotting began.

The ride to the hospital was silent—my husband not knowing what to say to me and fear of another loss choking my words.

Once I entered the Emergency Room, I was wheeled from place to place. It was all a blur, and felt like I was holding my breath for hours. So much for being able to exhale. I remember putting my clothes back on after an exam and a sonogram, then sitting in a small private waiting room. My very kind and gentle OB/GYN entered the room and told my husband and me that there was no longer a heartbeat in my womb. The baby had died. She retrieved some material about what I could expect to happen to my body in the next twenty-four to forty-eight hours.

But I'd named it and I claimed it! What's the deal, God?

A young African-American woman in a black pantsuit and clerical collar came in, sat across from us, and asked if we wanted her to pray. I bowed my head but didn't hear a thing; I shut it all out.

Surely this could not be happening again! There must be something about me that is not pleasing to God. But what about the people who mistreat children? Why are they getting the desire of my heart?

When we lived in Pennsylvania, I worked at the Sears Department store. While walking through the entertainment section, I glanced at a television and did a double take because I recognized the woman being interviewed on the news as the mother of one of my friends. She described finding a newborn baby in a purse hanging on a bathroom stall door. Wow, one degree of separation from someone on the news, but I only fleetingly thought about the baby. After my first miscarriage, news of babies discarded, abandoned, or even killed by their parents made me want to scream. How could they be so callous as to squander what so many others wanted—what I wanted? My rage was on a constant simmer, and from time to time it would boil over. *How could God be so unfair to me?*

"God's a safe-house for the battered, a sanctuary during bad times" (Psalms 9:9 MSG).

After our second loss, I had time to think as I unpacked in our new home. I considered some of the things I believed the Bible promised. The experiences of those whose stories were written seemed contrary to a life of ease and prosperity. No one was claiming, speaking, and naming what they wanted, and they were much more concerned about spreading the Gospel.

In the book of Acts, a man named Stephen was responsible for waiting tables and ensuring the often overlooked widows had enough to eat. The writer described Stephen as being full of faith, grace, and power. Yet, he was martyred for his faith, forgiving those who stoned him as he died.

Could God hold someone that close when they were in excruciating physical pain? Could His touch be real enough to comfort me in this place of devastation?

Now, I wasn't asking for things from a long-ago list—which suddenly seemed repellent and mocking. A first-class ticket to the moon couldn't touch my anguish. I needed my shattered heart to be mended.

While I mourned the previous images of a house full of children, I needed God to give me a new vision constructed from his love and care, not one of my own making from musicals and movies. My soul was in tatters when I called my parents and friends to inform them that I'd had another miscarriage. The feeling of shame for being the reason for other people's disappointment, for thinking I was less than a woman, was almost unbearable, and the help I longed for had to be real.

Restoration has been a process, and there hasn't been a formula that I could name and claim. The belief that no one will have trouble or difficulties seems naive to me now. In any life experience, there is fullness and famine; there is joy and suffering, delight and distress, and I was not exempt. This realization was central to my healing after my second loss. Sometimes, being quiet while looking out a window was a balm to my soul. Whenever I'd read about people who discovered what was really precious—health, life, joy, peace—after losing everything, I felt a kinship. One time as I sat in the drive-thru of a McDonald's, a song with lyrics from Psalms 121 came on the radio.

"I will lift my eyes to the hills, from whence cometh my help, my help cometh from the Lord, the Lord which made heaven and earth". I had never heard the song before, but it nearly reduced me to liquid form.

Healing came on tiptoes, barely making any noise—conversing with a friend, walking on a wooded path, or being inside on a rainy day with a cup of tea. My healing came little by little, but it did come...and is still coming twenty-five years later.

Everywhere I interact with people—church, work, reunions, holiday parties—inevitably the question is asked, "How many children do you have?" When I say, "None," most people can mask their surprise and keep a neutral expression. Others tilt their heads with sympathy, and say, "Aww..."

Four years ago, I was invited to speak at a church in Michigan and had a lovely time. Of course, "The question" came up quite a few times, and if someone wanted more information beyond my default answer of "none," they got nothing from me. After years of practice, my extraction skills from an awkward conversation could rival any escape artist. When we had a private moment, a friend told me, "I noticed every time someone asked if you had children, your head and shoulders drooped more each time." I was not aware of this until she pointed it out.

Philippians 4:12 (TLB) is a verse that makes me hopeful when I'm challenged to feel shame or pity about anything, not just because I don't have children. "I know how to live on almost nothing or with everything. I have learned the secret of contentment in every situation, whether it be a full stomach or hunger, plenty or want".

There are unfolding secrets in learning how to live contentedly. Just as healing can go as deep as the pain, the secret of contentment can flower in every circumstance, unfurling its petals to soothe and offer relief. Although contentment is specific for each person, because we are all different, I have observed it has a common starting point—gratitude, and thankfulness, for what you already have.

My gynecologist had been working with me to find out why I had the miscarriages and she discovered I had quite a few fibroids, but the good news was they could be removed. After coming up with a plan for surgery, I began to experience some very odd symptoms: sleeplessness, lightheadedness, palpitations, and hot flashes. She assured me that at thirty-eight years old, I was too young for menopause. But further testing proved I was in the one percent of women who start menopause before they turn forty—more soul-shattering news.

We didn't pursue adoption because I couldn't let myself be that vulnerable again concerning children. I needed time for God to remove the shrapnel from my heart and mend the fragmented pieces. My simple, perpetual prayer since that time has been, *God, help me*. Has it always been easy? No. A few years ago, the world became obsessed with the Octomom, a woman who'd had eight embryos implanted. Two of the biggest reality shows, *Jon and Kate Plus Eight* and *Twenty Kids and Counting*, revolved around the lives of families with multiple children. They were hard for me to watch.

God, help me.

There are days when I want to clutch bitterness and jealousy to my chest and hug them. But embracing those twin emotions would bend my personality into an unattractive shape and create a miserable life.

God, help me.

Every Mother's Day I have to make a decision to be happy for my friends who are mothers.

God, help me, and He does.

"My Presence will go with you, and I will give You rest." (Exodus 33:14 ESV)

I understand God's promises differently than I did when I was younger. It's not wrong to want nice things, but I can enjoy a meal in an upscale restaurant, or at Burger King. Travel is enjoyable, but a stroll in a park is great. My bullet lists were a thin disguise for my own avarice. Naming and claiming took time, energy, blank journals, and all but willing myself to get what I wanted from God. It brought no peace, no joy, and often inspired jealousy when I saw someone else get what I desperately wanted, and it made me question whether God loved me.

God's promises are full, expansive, delightful, and trustworthy. Each one is written in the pages of His Word. He tells us who He will be to us. And when life is painful, I let Him be my Enough.

Anyone who has reached adulthood knows that life brings the unexpected, but..."The Lord has promised that He will not leave us or desert us" (Hebrews 13:5 CEV).

Years ago, one of my younger cousins bit me on my thumb and it became infected. The doctor numbed my thumb and inserted a scalpel. He used a needle to shoot antibiotics deep into the wound. Over time my thumb healed, but the scar remained. When I accidentally hit it, it reminds me of the incident.

There is a healed-over tender spot on my wound of childlessness, but as heart-wrenching as an unfulfilled pregnancy can be, God has promised "He is near to the broken hearted and saves those who are crushed in spirit" (Psalms 34:18). Like the doctor's antibiotic injection into my thumb, God's promise to be near has entered my heart and gone as deep as the pain of an empty womb. "He heals the brokenhearted and bandages their wounds" (Psalms 147:3 MSG).

Kimball Honoré McNeal is an emerging creative nonfiction writer, industry blogger, and songwriter. She is a worship leader and Bible teacher, and in the final completion stage of a mini e-Book entitled *Thunderstorms in The Desert: How We Are Aging, Flourishing, & Lighting Up The World*. The full version is due out in late 2024.

An enthusiast of powerful storytelling, she co-facilitates *The Answer Is Write*, a writer's group based in North Carolina. She is the Marketing Director for Faith Journey Publishing.

Kim lives with her husband in Raleigh, NC, but remains a loyal daughter of the City of Brotherly Love and Sisterly Affection, Philadelphia, PA, and has a discerning palate for *authentic* cheese steaks, soft pretzels, and water ice.

Living Beyond the Mustard Seed Faith

"Through the LORD's mercies we are not consumed, Because His compassions fail not. They are new every morning; Great is Your faithfulness. 'The LORD is my portion,' says my soul, 'Therefore I hope in Him!'" (Lamentations 3:22-24 KJV).

Whenever I read this Scripture or hear a musical rendition of this verse, I usually cry. This scripture reminds me of the Lord's consistent faithfulness throughout my lifetime. I know He doesn't have to demonstrate His faithfulness the way He does so consistently, but I also know it is because of His great mercy that He does. Another song that profoundly affects me and causes my emotions to surface is CeCe Winans' version of the song "Goodness of God." There is a line in the song that proclaims, "All my life you have been faithful, all my life you have been so, so good..." which resonates with me because it is so true! All my life I have known God to be a faithful God. There are so many experiences, circumstances, and testimonies I could write about.

For several years, I've wanted to share this story of God's faithfulness in my finances. I don't want this to overshadow all the other times God has been faithful in other areas of my life, but this specific experience was humbling. It was one of the more memorable times I had to rely 100% on God. Not my family or friends, not my will, power, ability, or understanding. Just God.

Growing up, I knew I could depend on my parents to take care of me and help me with anything I needed. I was taught as a child to be faithful in my giving.

The giving Scripture we heard most often in church was Malachi 3:8-11 (KJV). "Will a man rob God? Yet ye have robbed me.

But ye say, 'Wherein have we robbed thee?' In tithes and offerings. Ye are cursed with a curse: for ye have robbed me, even this whole nation. Bring ye all the tithes into the storehouse, that there may be meat in mine house, and prove me now herewith, saith the LORD of hosts, if I will not open you the windows of heaven, and pour you out a blessing, that there shall not be room enough to receive it. And I will rebuke the devourer for your sakes, and he shall not destroy the fruits of your ground; neither shall your vine cast her fruit before the time in the field, saith the LORD of hosts."

From the time I started working my first job in the Summer Youth Program at about the age of fourteen, I understood the teaching. Initially, it placed me somewhere between fear and faith, but in any case, I was obedient. To be honest, it was initially because of fear, but as I matured, my "why should I pay tithes" became rooted in faith and trust in God. I continue to be faithful in my giving today. Ten percent—right off the top, every paycheck—as well as the above and beyond amounts like buying snacks and toys for the children's ministry and donating to each program or event we sponsor. I continue simply because I have experienced first-hand the blessings tied to tithing.

Even when I started working, if I didn't have enough to cover my bills, my parents helped me. They paid several months of my car insurance when I purchased my first car. It seemed they were an ever-present safety net. Today I am still grateful for all their sacrifices. However, as I grew older, I became more self-reliant.

For most of my life, I have been the type of person who has respected the importance of money and been very serious about my finances. Not that I haven't made mistakes, wasted money, or made bad decisions. But I had to balance my checkbook to the penny every month. I did not bounce checks or overdraft my account.

I didn't—still don't—like to play lottery games with money. I liked to make money, have money, and spend money. I didn't like to waste money, and I was confident that it was the solution to most of my problems. I felt like I would always be able to make more money, or I would find ways to make enough to fix anything. I believed money was one of the best, and sometimes the only, solution to whatever challenges I faced.

Although I was money conscious, I was never greedy or stingy. I was generous with my funds—when I wanted to be. On the other hand, I knew how to be frugal. Waste not, want not, as the saying goes. If it wasn't on sale, I probably wouldn't buy it. Take me straight to the sale rack! Overall, you could say, I tried to make sound decisions with my money. Sometimes those of us who tend to be a bit more careful about our spending will occasionally take certain liberties when we believe we have achieved a certain financial status, level of stability, or comfort. Presuming we have "arrived" at a particular financial status, we tend to splurge a little more, spend more than we should, or-pay a slightly higher price for items or services than we normally would. Let's face it, a level of wastefulness can easily creep in.

During this cycle of earning, saving, spending, splurging, giving, getting, I was still faithful in paying my tithes and offerings to the church.

Fast forward to 2013. My divorce was finalized, and the security of an extra income was gone. I was left with more debt than I should have had, and there was less income to apply toward that debt. I wracked my brain trying to find solutions to my financial dilemma. I found myself trying to work things out on my own. I tried to get a personal loan, and though my credit score was excellent, my debt-to-income ratio was too high. I considered seeking additional employment, but my daughter-in-law was battling heart failure and seemed to spend more time in the hospital than at home. I needed to help my son take care of their two small children. I looked for opportunities to work overtime at my job, but there wasn't much available, and again, the demands of my two grandchildren would make juggling extra hours difficult. Then I thought, *"Aha, I've got it! I will apply for a Home Equity Line of Credit* (HELOC)." That didn't work either. The value of my home was less than the amount I owed on the home loan at that time, so there was no equity available.

With few options available for relief, I depleted most of my savings and had to cash in my certificates of deposit to stay afloat and make ends meet. I found myself in a paycheck-to-paycheck situation, with a little bit of "robbing Peter to pay Paul" in between. In other words, I was praying and thought I was trusting God, but things weren't happening fast enough for me, so I tried to fix them on my own. I was impatient and tried to "help" God solve the problem. I learned I have to let God be God. Let Him do what He does best— work things out for our good (Romans 8:28).

Fast forward a few more years to about 2017.... The housing market began to improve, and there was now some equity in my home. Great news, right? Well, sort of. While I now had equity in my home, I could not borrow on that equity without the signature of my ex-husband. For anyone who has ever been through divorce, you might know the challenge I faced. I felt it was going to be next to impossible! How would I get my ex-husband to sign papers for me to get a Home Equity Line of Credit on a home he no longer lived in? Once again, I felt hopeless and with no options, or so I thought.

I was desperate, and I started to try to think of what it would take to get him to agree to sign the papers. I didn't like lying and cheating, and I certainly could not see myself sitting in a jail cell because of all of this, but I was so stressed! I was at my wits' end, and for the first time ever, I could not fix this one on my own. This was going to take a miracle, divine intervention, at least! As I continued to worry about my circumstances, unable to figure out a solution, I had to prepare for a trip to Seattle, Washington to attend a conference for my job.

One thing about traveling, it helps take my mind off whatever is going on in the moment—like temporarily leaving my troubles behind, making it feel like a brief vacation from the issues at hand. Unfortunately, troubles don't actually go away, do they? No, troubles are right there to greet you when you return.

Seattle was a beautiful city and the weather was amazing. It rained only one evening and then for just a brief period of time. The third day of the conference, I awoke to the beautiful, bright sunshine and there was a song in my heart: "God Will Take Care of You" by Walter Hawkins and the Love Center Choir. I had not heard this song in at least twenty years, but there I was singing this song as if I had just heard it yesterday on the radio—or my cell phone playlist. As I sang this song, I could feel the presence of God lifting my spirit and renewing my faith, washing away my worries, cares, and concerns about my financial woes. I remember thinking, *Yes, God has promised He will take care of me!* From that moment on, I knew everything would be alright, confirming that God would take care of everything! I didn't know how and I didn't know when, but I felt assured that it would be done. Why do we always feel like we need to know the why, when, what, and how of things, when all we really need to know is the Who? I began to thank God as I cried tears of joy and relief.

When I returned home, I called my ex-husband. I let him know the bank for the loan officer, and sign the required documents. He agreed to go, but the enemy began to sow negative thoughts in my mind, causing me to doubt. *He's not going to show up! Why should he help you?* Worry tried to return, but I had to trust the promises of God. I had to lean not on my own understanding and let God direct my path, work it out, and figure out the details.

I went to the bank to sign the documents and I let my ex-husband know to expect a call from the loan officer, and he would need to go into the bank and sign the required documents. The loan officer told me she would call me when everything had been completed. I left the bank assured *"only God can do it"*, whatever His "it" would happen to be, in this situation.

Later that afternoon, the bank called and said all the documents had been signed and my HELOC had been approved, and the money would be deposited into my account. Praise the Lord! Though my faith wavered, His faithfulness to me never did. God had my back all the time. I learned to let go of the control I thought I had and let God do things His way. I realized that God's solution is the best solution to every problem. He is the only one who knows the precise combination to unlock the door. He has and is the one and only key. Now I try my best to live each day, trusting God's promises in everything. It's challenging, but I try to wait for His direction, answers, solutions, and plans for my life. I can't afford to trust Him with some things but not others. I must trust Him with everything. Completely.

Just one more song, if I may. "Every word He's promised is true, What I thought was impossible, I've seen my God do, He's been faithful, faithful to me," are the lyrics to "He's Been Faithful" that tell me who God is.

He promised to never leave us, nor forsake us, and though we can't always see it or understand it, He is true to His Word. God is truly faithful!

Traci A. Coburn is a native of Colorado and is a University of Northern Colorado graduate with a Bachelor of Science Degree in Business Administration. She retired from the City and County of Denver after 34 years as an Internal Auditor.

Traci is a member of the Board of Directors and Treasurer for a local non-profit, STOP COVAD (Crimes of Violence and Discrimination), in Denver, Colorado.

A member of the Prince of Peace Temple, Church of God in Christ, in Aurora, Colorado, Traci's had the unique opportunity of being pastored by her grandfather, father, brother, and currently her son. She was recently elevated to the position of Assistant Pastor of the church. Traci is a licensed Evangelist Missionary in the Church of God in Christ, working actively on the local, state, and national levels.

She is the mother of two sons and has three grandchildren. Her hobbies include reading, watching documentaries, and dining with family and friends.

Witness to God's Faithful Promises

When I think about the promises in the word of God and how He has fulfilled them in my life, I am overwhelmed, not because of sadness or disparity; quite the contrary! God has shown Himself faithful in so many ways, I can hardly think of one without another one coming to mind.

To choose only one to share is quite challenging, but since I must, I'd like to recall the events of the morning of November 15, 2019. That was the day my life changed. It was 8:30 Friday morning, and I was preparing to go to my hair appointment as usual.

I called my husband for our morning embrace and to tell him good day before I set out. When he did not answer me, I thought he had already gone walking. I was in the living room and saw his sneakers in front of his favorite chair. So I walked around the house until I found him in the bathroom seated on the toilet.

I asked him to tell me his name, and he softly, almost breathed his name, "Kevin." He looked odd; his eyes seemed out of focus. I immediately called 911, and within minutes EMT and the fire truck were outside our home. They took his blood pressure, which was 200 over 190—or some outrageous number. My husband was quickly whisked into the ambulance, and I hastily got into our car to follow.

On my way to the hospital, I heard the spirit of the Lord say to me, "This sickness is not unto death." I wondered why I would hear these words. My husband had been hospitalized before for similar medical situations; why should this be any different? The routine had become familiar; arrive at the hospital, be directed to the ER bed he was in, sit for several hours or overnight for tests and observation. He'd be released, then we would go home. So why did the words come?

Little did I know God was preparing me for what I would encounter upon my arrival. Standing at the admittance desk, I said I was there for Kevin Thorne. This time, instead of being directed to the bed he was in, they asked me to have a seat. Have a seat? Did I get to the hospital before the ambulance? What was going on? After a while someone came into the lobby, called my name and identified himself as a 'Spiritual Guide.' He then asked me to go with him. We walked into a dimly lit room and sat down. "Your husband is in serious condition. The doctor will meet you here in a moment."

The neurosurgeon, Dr. Garner, entered the room. He explained they had done a cat scan and found Kevin had experienced a brain bleed; an operation would be needed immediately. As his wife, I needed to give permission for them to do the surgery. I was very calm throughout the conversation because the Lord told me while I was in the car that my husband's sickness was not his demise.

The Spiritual Guide looked at me a bit strangely and asked if I was okay. I told him I was fine. I think he was a bit surprised that I was not out of my head, crying, or yelling in despair. During this time I was prayerful, grateful, and patient regarding what would happen next. In our relationship with God, I've learned that if we listen to Him, He prepares us for any situation that may arise and otherwise catch us off our guard.

After realizing that my husband would not go home for a while, I did not want to be far from his side. Especially when I did not know what would happen after surgery. I went home and packed some clothes and my toiletry bag.

We had left the house so abruptly that morning, I walked in the house, decided to do a little cleaning up and on my way into the living room, I stopped to pick up Kevin's sneakers. They weren't there. I knew I had seen them that morning. The sneakers had prompted me to look for Kevin in the first place, noting he had not gone out walking. Going into our bedroom, I passed his closet, there were the sneakers. But that couldn't be! I saw them in the living room... "Are not all angels ministering spirits sent to serve those who will inherit salvation" (Hebrews 1:14 NIV). That was the Scripture that resonated within me. Angels are always on assignment. I believe an angel was assigned to make sure the sneakers were planted in plain sight to alert me my husband was in need. I finished packing what was necessary and returned to the hospital to stay with him.

One thing is certain, the Lord promised He would take care of my husband. I did not know what that would look like or how it would play out. The only thing I understood is that He promised Kevin would live.

I had no idea it would mean my husband would be in the hospital from November 2019 until May 2020. He lay in the bed for many weeks, not saying a word, but I played worship music in the room every day. Right by Kevin's ear my phone played Scripture verses of healing. We listened to Gloria Copeland as she taught about healing and the Word of God. We had the entire atmosphere saturated with God's presence. Since Kevin's room had only a curtain for a wall, those walking by experienced the presence of the Lord as well. We prayed, sang, and trusted God for healing.

When it came to my husband's healing, one of the things I had to realize was that if we expected to receive anything from the Lord, we had to come to Him and be specific. Just like Jesus when he raised

Lazarus from the dead. If He had simply said, "Come forth!", all the dead folk would have come forth. I became very aware of what God wanted of me. "Trust and obey, for there is no other way to be happy in Jesus, but to trust and obey" (one of my favorite songs by recording artist, Don Moen).

I was concerned about who came into our space, careful to have only those who believed that healing is our portion come into the room. We spoke the promises of God over Kevin daily. Even though he was not saying anything, he could definitely hear what was being said. When we choose to believe, we are confident in what the Word of God says. Daily I trusted the process and watched God work in my husband's body. My heart became more sensitive to the Spirit of God. My prayers became more focused and specific.

Listening for the voice of the Lord was important to the healing of my husband's body. Every day my heart became fixed, trusting in the Lord. My mind was being nourished by the Word of God. I had healing Scriptures and inspirational music soaking and soothing the atmosphere.

Our room was the first one you saw when you came into the NICU (Neuro Intensive Care Unit) area. As I now look back on that, I am reminded that every person who walked in the NICU had to pass by our space first. I can recall, on several occasions, hearing people say there was such peace emanating from our room. They often commented on the music that was playing–how it was soothing. I see now that God was permeating that entire area with peace.

Our children live out of state, and it was hard to make those calls. However, before I called them, I prayed they would not be alone and that they would be covered with the Presence of God.

Kevin, our oldest, was with his girlfriend when we spoke. Kennedy Elayne, was with her Godmother when I called her. Both of our children wanted to come immediately, but I told them to take their time because we had a bit of a road to go, and at this point there was nothing they could do. Kevin's girlfriend drove with him when they came to spend time at the hospital during the Thanksgiving holiday. You see our Father is so faithful that He hears even the most simple prayers.

The nurses were drawn to Kevin's room. They would come in just to talk and have a reprieve from their work. I remember one nurse was going through something, and in the middle of what was happening with Kevin, I was blessed with an opportunity to minister to her. She shared with me some very private issues, and was a little hesitant, saying that this was not professional. I remember her turning away from me, because her eyes were filled with tears. I had given her words of encouragement. She wiped her eyes and told me that what I said was just what she needed. She was so grateful. One gentleman shared his heart with me, and wept as he said he was jealous of my faith. Others shared their stories with me about heartache, and they were encouraged by God working through me.

God promises that if we seek first the kingdom and His righteousness, all other things will be added (Matthew 6:33). I trust in the God who sees, hears, and knows all. He continues to show Himself strong in our lives, and I am thankful that He keeps His Word.

Just when I think I am finished, I am reminded of another fulfillment of the promises of God. It was a few weeks before I knew my husband would be coming home. There was not a plan in place at the time. All I knew was nurses, physical, occupational, and speech therapists would come to the home several times a week.

But what I did not know was how would I care for my husband. What would it look like? I had no idea! One thing I do know is that our children were phenomenal! When their dad came home, each of them were able to spend several months with us because it was during the Covid pandemic, and they were able to work remotely. They helped their father as he was exercising and learning to do household chores again. I cannot begin to tell you how thankful I am for our two world-changer young adults! They absolutely are the most wonderful gift God blessed us with!

Our daily time spent in His presence studying, memorizing, and obeying the Word of God, plus following the leading of the Holy Spirit, deepens our ability to hear Him when He speaks. It is in the everyday, moment by moment as we open our hearts to the Father that He reveals Himself and His many attributes. When I did not know what the outcome would be, our Father in heaven already had the plan. Our Father watches over us to keep us. He forever keeps His promises.

He gave us precious promises, and as we lean into His Word, we can access those promises on a daily basis.

Darlene Thorne, MDiv, is the CEO of A Heart After the Father, LLC, and serves as a Caregiver's Coach/Mentor. Her mission is to influence change in women ministry leaders, teaching them how to practice positive, personal self-care through body, soul, and spirit.

As an international speaker, Darlene delivers life-impacting messages at conferences and facilitating workshops and symposiums. Featured on television and radio, Darlene helps others to focus on walking in total freedom and authenticity.

A published author, Darlene has written several books including contributing in two anthologies. Each of her books have been a part of Darlene's journey in leading others to deepen their relationship with God.

She and her husband, Kevin Thorne, serve together as pastors at Renewal Community Church in Clayton, NC. They have two world changer young adults, Kevin, II and Kennedy Elayne. You may contact Darlene Thorne via IG at linktr.ee/Ladydarlene.

Faith, Legacy, and God's Promises

My dad died almost four years ago after a long battle with Alzheimer's. What I regret the most is that I wasn't able to be with him when he passed. In all truthfulness, I don't think I will ever find comfort or peace about that, even though I know as a believer our life continues eternally with Christ without pain or suffering. I know full well my dad is in a better place. I tell myself that and have been told the same, but, the regret still takes place within that meant to be a comfort. As I have wrestled with that regret, I have searched high and low for some promise from God that I embrace. What I discovered, though, were these words from Hebrews: "Faith shows the reality of what we hope for; it is the evidence of things we cannot see." All the people we read about in this chapter died still believing what God had promised them. They did not receive what was promised, but they saw it all from a distance and "welcomed it" (Hebrews 11:1, 13 NLT).

I grieved for my dad because he had worked so hard to survive; he had beaten the odds and survived! In fact, you could say that he thrived and continued to thrive. But at the age of 65, Alzheimer's began to chip away at the amazing retired life I had hoped for him—what I felt was promised to him for all of his hard work. This was the time my dad was supposed to rest, enjoy, and tell me all of his stories. But his memory started going gradually, then like a landslide. He could no longer recognize my brother, me, or his grandchild who was so much like him. On the outside, he looked like my dad, but inside, it felt like he was already gone.

On the day he died, I was 3,000 miles away celebrating my mother-in-law's birthday. I felt heartbroken, angry, frustrated, and numb all at the same time. I'm still not sure what you are supposed to feel when someone you love dies, but it seems typical for many different feelings to overwhelm you at the same time. Even though I had begun my grieving process as his Alzheimer's progressed, the news of his passing hit me in a new way, because now the hope—no matter how small it was—that somehow his Alzheimer's would be cured died with him. Now I had to let go of that hope and trust the promise of eternal life in Christ where there would not be any more pain, suffering, or tears.

Throughout the years before my dad died, I had helped my mom to clean out their house so that they could downsize. As I was going through all their things, I discovered many letters that my dad had written to James and Phyllis Hunter. The Hunters were my dad's lifeline who eventually became family. My dad was orphaned during the Korean War. A church in Toronto, Canada sponsored a child—my dad. The Hunters were first introduced to my dad through that sponsorship, and when the sponsorship with the church ended, the Hunters continued it and stayed in touch with my dad. They wrote letters back and forth for years and years. When my dad met my mom, married, and immigrated to the States, they visited the Hunters in Canada. My dad essentially became their fourth son, and I grew up knowing the Hunters as my paternal grandparents. Eventually, the letters they stopped writing to my dad became letters they started writing to my brother and me until they passed.

After the Hunters passed, my dad received back all the letters that he had written to them, which they had lovingly kept in careful condition. It was such a gift, not only to my dad, but to me as well. As I opened each letter and read them, I discovered the earnest hopes and dreams of my dad—the promises that he knew were for him. English was not his heart language; however, my dad expressed his heart so beautifully in these letters. It was evident to me that my dad, even with all his hardships, had a solid faith that believed in a future which was promised to him. I don't know exactly when my dad encountered Jesus or his faith, but I did know that his faith was strong and bold. The letters revealed that, like those described in the book of Hebrews, my dad saw his promises from a distance and welcomed them.

The future my dad saw was one where his children did better than he did. It was a future secured in deep faith. It was a future that saw the next generation of our family continuing to thrive. It was a future where women were seen as equals to men, both spiritually speaking and in society. Growing up in a highly patriarchal society, he saw how his younger sister could not further her education beyond elementary school because girls and women were not as valued as boys or men. It was a future where the impossible could become reality. Even with his engineering mind, my dad was a big dreamer, and he envisioned all sorts of futures I am now living. He died believing all the things God had promised him because he had seen them from a distance. I believe this is the legacy of faith he has left for me. For my dad, I am the promises fulfilled and being fulfilled.

So much has happened in the past four years since my dad died, and every year, I wish he were here so that I could show him, tell him, and celebrate with him. My dad sensed my call from God before I did, and I wish so desperately he could come and hear me preach at church. As an Asian American woman, growing up in a traditional, immigrant church, I did not think that it was possible for me to become a pastor or to preach in a main worship service. But my dad knew the road ahead of me had already been paved to make something seemingly impossible for me possible. Every dream I chase after, which becomes a reality, is the blossoming of the promises my dad had seen.

His letters to the Hunters revealed the promises my dad felt God had made to him...and all those promises were within my brother and me.

My dad saw the glimpses of it as he raised us and did his best to parent, although he was living in a completely different world than what he had known. There was no reference point or guiding line for my dad—for along with my mom, he had to walk by faith in all aspects of life. He often prayed and encouraged us quietly, often going unnoticed. But when I looked into my dad's eyes, even during his battle with Alzheimer's, I saw his clear and unwavering earnestness and sincerity. I knew somewhere deep inside him, he knew who I was and this is what I needed. And my dad was patient; he knew that his promises from God would be fulfilled in time. What a legacy to leave behind! Because of his legacy, my own faith has grown. I have a deeper and better understanding that faith is the reality of what we hope for and the evidence of what we cannot see.

I am the promises fulfilled for my dad. The beauty of this realization for me is my small comfort in my regret of not being by his side when he passed. Even before his Alzheimer's, my dad had already seen God's promises from a distance and welcomed them. His faith is the promise I feel God has given to me. It has paved the road in front of me, even though I may not always know which way the road is going. I can be sure God will always be next to me, just as God was with my dad. The words of Psalms 23 that we read at my dad's funeral rang true and was the testament of my dad's life: "The Lord is my shepherd; I have all that I need. He lets me rest in green meadows; he leads me beside peaceful streams. He renews my strength. He guides me along right paths, bringing honor to his name. Even when I walk through the darkest valley, I will not be afraid, for you are close beside me.

Your rod and your staff protect and comfort me. You prepare a feast for me in the presence of my enemies. You honor me by anointing my head with oil. My cup overflows with blessings. Surely your goodness and unfailing love will pursue me all the days of my life, and I will live in the house of the Lord forever," (Psalms 23, NLT).

These are the promises that God has given to you and to me. The legacy of my dad and those who came before us are the testament and evidence of what we cannot see. It is the hope and trust we can have even if our promises are not fulfilled before we die. The past four years of working through my own grief have brought me to this realization; whatever it is you might be wrestling with right now or have wrestled with, my prayer and hope is that God will tangibly be close beside you, renewing, strengthening, honoring, blessing, and pursuing you. May you be the embodiment of the promises fulfilled of our heavenly God.

Phyllis Myung is a pastor, communicator, and writer. Originally from Seattle, Washington, Phyllis currently lives in a suburb outside of Boston, with her husband, teenager, and an adorable rescue dog named Cookie. Phyllis presently serves at Great Road Church as the Next Gen pastor. She immensely enjoys working with children, youth, and their families. In addition to her pastoral role, Phyllis is also the Director of Engagement for the Asian American Christian Collaborative. She blogs occasionally (the napkinhoarder.com) but is always on the hunt for the best burger in the world, and her happy place is wherever the ocean is.

Called to Ministry and Hearing God's Voice

Joshua 21:45 (NLT) says, "Not a single one of all the good promises the Lord had given to the family of Israel was left unfulfilled; everything he had spoken came true."

God is amazing! God is faithful! He *will* keep His promises! I want to share how God fulfilled several of these promises in my life and why Psalms 91 is one of my favorites to this day.

Psalms 91 has a lot of powerful promises.

- "I will rescue you..."

- "I will protect you..."

- "I will answer you..."

- "I will be with you in trouble..."

- "I will deliver you..."

- "I will honor you..."

- "I will satisfy you with long life..."

- "I will show you my salvation..."

While reading these verses, I understood and experienced this truth like never before.

In 1993, after our oldest daughter Jaylun was born, something changed inside me. I began to desire more of God. I felt compelled to read more and diligently seek the face of God; I wanted more of Him in my life! I had given my life to Christ at an early age. I knew Him but wasn't nurturing my relationship with Him. Big difference!

Over the next five years I began seeking God and getting to know Him more intimately. In August of '98, my husband David and I attended a revival at a local church. As the guest evangelist finished preaching, she gave an altar call, then said, "If anyone needs prayer, come down to the altar." We both went down to the front for prayer.

The evangelist began to pray for the others, then started to walk in our direction, but she never got close enough to touch us. Neither of us had any idea what had happened. All I know is when I came to, I was on the floor, and my husband was lying beside me. We had never experienced anything like that before. I would later find out we had encountered the Holy Spirit. David didn't have another experience like that anymore during the entire week of the revival, but I had that marvelous experience six more times!

After such an astounding encounter with the Holy Spirit that week, the enemy began to attack in ways I can't even begin to explain. He presented lies and convinced me to believe things that weren't true.

The mind is powerful, and it can become the enemy's battlefield. He wants to take the battle into your mind because that's where he tries to do his best work. Romans 12:2 (NASB) says, "Be not conformed to this world but be transformed by the renewing of your mind, then you may prove what that good, acceptable and perfect will of God is for your life."

God wants us to strengthen our minds with His Word, so we can be strong in the power of His might and know what His perfect will is for our lives. The enemy seeks to imprison us in our minds with his lies.

That week, after my encounter with the Holy Spirit, the enemy convinced me I couldn't touch our children because the anointing on me was too strong. He said, "If you touch them, they will die!" I was running from my kids and locking myself in the bathroom. I was also seeing things that weren't there. One day as I was changing my daughter's diaper, I began to see what looked like worms crawling under her skin! It became so bad, David considered committing me to a mental institution. But during it all, God protected me!

One night while sitting at my kitchen table, exhausted from the daily spiritual attacks of the enemy that week, my Bible lay open on the table, and a breeze went through our kitchen. The pages turned and then stopped at Psalms 91! I was unfamiliar with that psalm but desperate for some relief, so I started to read it.

"Whoever dwells in the shelter of the Most High will rest in the shadow of the Almighty. I will say of the Lord, 'He is my refuge and my fortress, my God, in whom I trust. Surely, he will save you from the fowler's snare and from the deadly pestilence'" (Psalms 91:1-3 NIV).

I read the entire psalm and highlighted what made my spiritual baby kick. I looked at every promise, underlining them in red, and then searched the verses to see the conditions. *What am I supposed to do? God is sure to do His part, but what about me?* The first verse read, "Dwell in the secret place." I had little to no idea what that meant at that time. *What did it mean to dwell in "the secret place?" What secret place?* I read it over and over and over again, and as I read, I started accepting what I was reading.

I believe I entered the secret place, because I could feel the weight of the enemy's oppression get lighter and the prison doors he had built in my mind begin to swing open. God kept His promise and rescued me from the snare of the fowler! The enemy is not afraid of our words, but he is afraid of the Word of God, spoken in faith coming from the tongue of a Holy Spirit-filled believer.

The seven days I spent in turmoil felt like seven months, but I felt closer to God than ever. I could clearly hear his voice; it almost sounded audible.

Have you ever had someone you know call you, and because you're pretty sure you know what they want—and it's something you're not 100% sure you're ready to give—you don't answer the phone? But they keep calling?

A few weeks later, after everything had calmed down with things almost back to normal, God called me into ministry! He kept calling, and calling, and calling. He said, "Valissa, love my people, feed my people, teach my people."

What if I don't know the answer to a Bible question? You know, people expect ministers to know every Word of the Bible.

Will I face opposition?

What if I teach something wrong?

I was a member of the choir at that time and ministering in song was what I felt comfortable doing and wasn't sure about taking on anything else. I said, *"God, just let me keep singing. I'll sing for you, but don't ask me to preach or teach your word. I'm comfortable right where I am."* If the enemy oppressed me like he did before I answered the call, how much more will he try to oppress me if I accept the call?

What if? What if? What if?

I started doubting whether I had even heard the voice of God myself. With every concern I had, God would refer me back to His promises in Psalms 91. Well, guess what? I accepted the call!

The Scriptures He had revealed to me at my kitchen table, Psalms 91, became mine. It was my love letter because it contained promises to *me* from God.

In Psalms 91, God promised me, if I dwelt in the secret place with Him, I would abide under His shadow and He would be my refuge, my fortress, my God, and in Him I could trust. As I studied this psalm, I became more confident that God would never leave me or forsake me and that He would protect me. So, I said "yes" to the call to ministry.

In my home church, there had only been one female who had ever been ordained as a minister. I would be the second in over 125 years. I went to the leadership and was excited about my decision and shared what I believed God was asking me to do, but there was little to no response. Surprisingly, this announcement wasn't met with mutual excitement. There were stares, confused facial expressions, and silence. I faced doubt and negativity from other people. I couldn't understand why only a few were excited about the call on my life. I knew that being a minister of the gospel had its challenges, but I never expected that many of the challenges I'd face would be because I'm a woman. I have kept this matter concealed and locked away for over 25 years, hesitating to speak or write about it, but now, I believe the time has come to be open.

Shortly after, people started calling me from all over North Carolina asking me to speak at various church events and programs.

A year later, as I was speaking at one of the events, someone recorded the service, and it ended up in the hands of my pastor.

Eventually, I was allowed to preach my initial sermon. I wanted to share it with everyone, my family, and church family. Until recently, only my husband and a select number of people knew about my entire journey. Things are slightly different now for women preachers and pastors than 25 years ago. One thing I've discovered is that my experiences and what I learn are meant to mold and shape me, but they're also for me to share with others, to help mold and encourage each one to walk in God's will for their lives. I tell this story to inspire people to continually renew their minds as instructed in Romans 12:2 (NASB), "...Be transformed by the renewing of your mind," so we can see transformation in those who follow Christ.

God has been faithful. He has been my refuge, my fortress, and I know I can trust Him. The enemy has set a multitude of snares, but God has delivered me out of them all. He has ordered His angels to keep me lifted, so that I don't even dash my foot against a stone.

Before, during, and after I accepted the call, God was there. He has been with me. Even after God showed me all He would do through me, the places I would preach, and the books I would write, instead of releasing me to pursue those things, He asked me to homeschool my kids, which I did for 25 years. I didn't understand this instruction because I was ready—or so I thought—for what He had shown me. Once again Psalms 91 offered me comfort. Verse 2 states, "I will say of the Lord, 'He is my refuge and my fortress, my God, in whom I trust'" (NASB). I might not always understand, but I learned I must trust the Lord.

The specific call on my life is to teach God's Word with simplicity so that even a child can understand it. What better way to show me how to teach God's Word with simplicity than to train me by allowing me to home-educate our children?

God will fulfill His promises to you; just trust, believe, and do your part.

Answer the call! Whenever, however, it comes.

Answer the call! Despite the obstacles, you think you may face.

Answer the call even if you're scared!

Answer the call if it looks hard!

Answer the call and change your life forever.

Answer the call and trust the plans God has for your life.

Numbers 23:19 (NLT) says, "God is not a man, so he does not lie. He is not human, so he does not change his mind. Has he ever spoken and failed to act? Has he ever promised and not carried it through?" The answer to both questions is an unequivocal "No." He has never promised and not carried through.

I've continued to find peace in the promises of Psalms 91 at every turn. He has fulfilled and continues to fulfill every promise to me and my family, and I know beyond a shadow of a doubt He will fulfill every promise to you as well. Answer the call!

Valissa Moore is the author of eight books. She consistently receives invitations to share the gospel and minister in song and has recorded CD albums. Her specific calling is to teach the gospel with such simplicity even a child could understand it.

She hosts a conference called "Renewed and Transformed" to help women and men and facilitates a virtual, life-changing training called "Meet Me at the Well." Valissa is also the host of a weekly Personal Development training.

Together, she and her husband host an annual couple's conference called "Beyond the Veil."

Valissa Moore and her husband, David, are the senior pastors of Reaping the Harvest Christian Church in Garner, North Carolina. Their ministry also helped establish Reaping the Harvest Christian Center in Kisii County, Kenya, and, the New Restoration Conference Ministries in Texas is under their ministry. Valissamoore.com

God's Promise, Beyond What I Can See

"A promise is a cloud; fulfillment is rain." – Anonymous

"Wherefore, seeing we also are compassed about with so great a cloud of witnesses, let us lay aside every weight, and the sin which doth so easily beset us, and let us run with patience the race that is set before us, looking unto Jesus the author and finisher of our faith, who for the joy that was set before him endured the cross despising the shame, and is set down at the right hand of the throne of God" (Hebrews 12:1-2, KJV).

I grew up deeply rooted in Christianity. I knew God from stories, songs, and testimonies from the saints. Throughout my life, through God's Word, the messages from this cloud of witnesses have flowed down to me, sometimes in single drops or as a steady stream of rain. However, there are other times when the message impacts my life in the form of a life-altering, raging storm.

The cloud of witnesses, as described in the book of Hebrews, speaks of saints who have passed away and now metaphorically surround those who believe in Christ. The witnesses are those who believed and received the promises of God by faith. My heart hears them as they whisper to me of fulfilled promises, answered prayers, and completed destinies. Their message is always the same: 'God is faithful.'

Our first home was on 25th Street in North Philadelphia. Ten to twelve row houses lined the block on both sides. During the late summer months, the city heat was so intense the kids on the block often waited until after dinner, but just before the streetlights came on, to go out and play. The boys would play street ball; the girls would play Jacks or Double Dutch or sit on the stoop getting their hair braided or corn rowed. Some elders would be on their porches rocking in their chairs, enjoying the cool evening breeze and watching it all.

It was during this time I would run my race. I ran it all by myself at only four years old. Boy, was I fast! I would dash up and down the street with vigor, passing each house door, the elders, and all the kids. I would hear kids say, "Look at Cookie go!" The elders would ask, "Where are you going so fast?" or "What, isn't this your tenth time down this block?"

I would run so fast, I soared down North 25th Street straight into my own world where I was the star of the show. I ran up and down that block at full speed, again and again, until I fell to the ground, exhausted but satisfied.

Even back then, I would stare into the sky and sense the stars, the sun, and the high noctilucent clouds were all watching me run and cheering me onto the finish. My mother would peek out the door a time or two to warn, "Not too fast now, slow down, Cookie" or "Be careful."

My mother always kept a watchful eye at home, and daily prayed for her children. My siblings and I grew up in somewhat of a bubble. As an adult, I often mentioned in conversations how we were sheltered. My mom would correct me and say that we were 'covered.'

Ours was a household where Jesus Christ, 'the crucified and risen Savior,' was at the center of every family function. I grew up a PK (Preacher's Kid) and PGK (Preacher's Grandkid). My uncle, as well as my father's first cousin, were also both ministers of the Gospel. So, naturally, I was flooded with stories, Bible verses, and testimonies attesting to the faithfulness of God. We children learned those verses and recited them all year, not just on Easter and Christmas.

At home, my mom read the same stories to us from her large vintage Holy King James red letter edition Regency Bible. I also heard the same stories in Sunday school, early morning service, afternoon service, evening service, Wednesday Bible study, Friday night prayer service, during revivals, Gospel concerts, and New Year's Eve services.

From Adam and Eve to John the Revelator, I listened and learned each of their stories for years; stories of endurance, patience, fortitude, and trust in God. I also imagined that they were expecting something from me.

No one could tell me I did not know God. What? I knew him and His Son, and I had the bloodline to prove it, didn't I? I confessed the sinner's prayer asking for forgiveness of my sins and for Jesus to come into my heart. I also accepted Christ as my personal Savior in the tradition of things and was baptized by my father at age ten. My name was written in the Book of Life, I was on my way to heaven, and all was settled.

As I grew older, graduated high school, and went to college, I broke away from my family's gaze and started doing my own thing. My mother called it 'running the streets.' I called it walking to my own beat.

With college came new experiences and experiments with drinking alcohol, boys, new and different philosophies, and religions. I still considered myself saved but somehow rationalized my behavior based on the idea that "God knows my heart." I created my own theology that conveniently left off the Scripture found in Jeremiah 17:9 (KJV) that says, "The heart is deceitful above all things and desperately wicked. Who can know it?" Many of the ideas I tinkered with did not seem to conflict with Christianity outwardly. The most interesting ideas were those semi-Christian concepts that removed the truth of Christ, declining to mention Jesus Christ as the risen and living Savior.

I discovered ideas declaring Jesus was a great prophet or someone worthy of a positive uplifting quote. I was entangled in so many different ideologies that I started to side eye the Bible and the Apostle Paul for a number of reasons, including its so-called misogyny or its treatment of the topic of slavery. I reached a point where the Bible no longer seemed relevant to me for study, and I ended up trading in the Apostle Paul for Jean Paul Sartre and others like him. I'd become an academic and relied on what could be proven through the senses.

Consequently, my spiritual life took a back seat. I had entered a very different race—running my life on my own. I believed I was the captain of my ship, the master of my soul.

"There is a way which seemeth right to a man; But the end thereof are the ways of death" (Proverbs 14:12 KJV).

Years go by, and as in any race of endurance, the terrain is not always smooth, the weather may be less than ideal, resources may dwindle, things fall apart, the center cannot hold, and people die. On December 26, 2012, my mother, Ella Ford Honoré, passed away. She was my first Bible teacher and so much more. It has been 11 years since her death. The nuances of our deeply layered, dynamic, and complicated relationship are still being unraveled.

Despite everything about our relationship, my mother was the person I could completely count on to 'be there.' Anytime I had an issue or felt like I was facing some insurmountable difficulty, I would go to my mother, and she was there. She was there for me when I became pregnant at nineteen, unwed, and still in college.

When she got wind of the news, she got in her car, rode up to my school, and barged into my dorm room, and we had it out right there in front of all the resident aides, the girls living on my floor, and all of the visiting parents. We were loud. She was screaming. I was crying and horrified, but she was there. When I got pregnant yet again at twenty-two, my mom was utterly disappointed that I was still unwed and expecting a second child. However, she did not desert me but continued praying and believing I would get it together.

My mother was there for every graduation, when I received a full scholarship to attend graduate school, and she was there when I threw it all away. I was involved in an abusive relationship with my daughters' father for a while. It was my mother who convinced me to leave without uttering a word. Eventually, when I finally left, she was there to help me to pick up the pieces. She gave me scripture to read and prayed for me. Her favorite Scripture was Proverbs 3:5-6 (KJV), "Trust in the Lord with all thine heart; and lean not to thine own understanding. In all thy ways acknowledge him, and He shall direct thy paths." She had the faith of God for me when I had none for myself.

When my mom died and joined the cloud of witnesses, I knew she had finished her race. Her death caused me to crash and fall—hard, although it was a gradual descent. Alcohol became my crutch. From late 2012 through late 2016, alcohol became a 24-hour, all-consuming, full-blown addiction. It replaced my prayers and Bible verses. Instead of the Bible, I grabbed the bottle. At the apex of my addiction, I drank from the moment I woke up until I went to sleep. I drank at work, on the train, in the car, and even in church. I became a sad joke to my co-workers, acquaintances, so-called friends, and sadly, even some of the church folk. I was so lost and in such pain; alcohol kept me from feeling it.

My strategic plan for each day centered around when and where I drank and the location of the nearest liquor store. There were days when I left work and did not go home and my family would search for me. They would find me sleeping in my car or walking the streets in oblivion. I was a deeply grieved, selfish, careless ticking time bomb. I lost weight, started getting sick, had two DUI accidents, was arrested twice, lost my house, all credibility, and was close to losing my job.

I was disgusted by my actions and full to the brink with shame, but that did not stop me. Numerous times I tried to stop drinking, by my own strength and power, and failed each time. I bought into the lie of 'just one more drink and I am done,' knowing that for someone like me who is plagued with alcoholism, one drink is too many and a thousand is not enough.

Despite it all, there was still the feeling that this was not 'it' for me. In the back of my mind were remembrances of the scripture about the cloud of witnesses, cheering me on, and waiting for me to do 'something.'

I am not sure how it happened. I do know that there was something in me that caused me to start fighting back. I started listening to old hymns I had not listened to in years. I would go on YouTube and listen to all the sermons I could find. I listened to gospel music. I listened to music that edifies the spirit. It was music I had stopped listening to years ago. I started reading the Bible for the first time in years, and I prayed without ceasing. The inner working of the Spirit is a mystery.

"The Lord is near to the broken hearted and saves the crushed in spirit" (Psalms 34:18 KJV). I read so much from Christian leaders and pastors online who spoke of the transformation of the heart and the work of the Holy Spirit.

Ah, yes! The Spirit of God is often symbolized as a cloud in scripture. I learned there is work the Spirit performs when He takes residence in the believer's heart. Understanding the work and presence of the Spirit of God does not come from book knowledge of Christ, but is from a personal relationship with Christ.

YouTube influencer Mavis Dibs on her channel, Undiluted Words, put it this way. "The Bible becomes the Word of God when taken up by the Holy Spirit, otherwise it is a manual the devil can quote."

Wow—was that how I read the Bible all these years? I meditated day and night on every Scripture I read and every song, prayer, and testimony I heard. A slow and steady accumulation started to occur in my heart and spirit.

I experienced an incredible desire for God. I desired intimacy with Him and began reading God's Word, allowing every verse to penetrate and change my heart. I no longer just read Scripture; I began to live it. I began to understand that my battle for sobriety required the Spirit of God and the struggle would not be won by my might or my power but by God's Spirit.

"For the weapons of our warfare are not carnal but mighty through the pulling down of strongholds" (2 Corinthians 10:4-5 ESV). My spirit was growing and gaining strength. The key to my sobriety was in reach. I simply needed to have enough faith to open the door and walk through.

Like my descent, my restoration was also gradual. I was still drinking but, now I was fighting back with power that was not of my own. No more carelessly wallowing in my pain.

Although I was gaining strength in spirit, my terrible habit kept me bound. A day of reckoning would come on October 13, 2016. While on the job, highly intoxicated, the office Assistant District Administrator confronted me with the truth regarding my behavior. She took me into her office, looked me in the eye, and said, "You need help."

Of course, I denied what was plain for all to see. The jig was up. I was devastated and relieved. That evening I went home and cried my heart out, praying for deliverance. Finally, I stopped running and I surrendered completely to Almighty God, and His infinite wisdom, Jesus Christ, and wholeheartedly acknowledged that I could not run this race of life without His Spirit.

The very next day, I fully accepted the promises of God and stepped out on faith. I entered Livengrin Addiction Recovery Center for alcoholism. I stayed at the facility for 30 days and was subsequently released.

Not drinking alcohol for the past 30 days, the hard part would begin, or so I initially believed. *Where would I get the power to stay sober forever? Where was that wonder-working power we sang about in church?* By God's grace, I believed His promise for my continued sobriety.

Initially, there was just a trickle. Then there was a steady flow and finally a bursting forth all around me of Christian brothers and sisters holding me up, praying for me. They began surrounding me at church, work, and my meetings. Those witnesses to God's promises were always there, encouraging me to step out in faith and to run the race set before me.

God honored my faith and fulfilled his promise. For the past six years and three months, I have remained sober. I have put away wine and spirits and instead am joyfully filled with the Spirit of God. My inner witness has taken up residence and fills me with rivers of living water.

For far too long, I remained that kid from North Philly who was content with merely running up and down the same block, repeating mistakes, tripping, and calling time out. God has called me to become more significant and to grow. I am learning to pace myself, knowing the race is not for the swift but to those who endure until the end, and to run with zeal, perseverance, and patience.

There have been many more promises I have looked to God to fulfill, and He has answered every one of them. I am now happily married. I have peace and joy again. I have taken on new roles at my job and am using the gifts He has given me for His glory. I know there are so many more promises for which I am believing God. I rest on the words found in Habakkuk 2:3 (KJV). "For the vision is yet for an appointed time, but at the end it shall speak and not lie; thought it tarry, wait for it; because it will surely come, it will not tarry."

Finally, my heart waits in great expectation for the promise of our Lord and Savior, Jesus Christ. For the day will come when all shall see Him as He is and witness the return of the King of Kings in a cloud. "Behold, He is coming with the clouds and every eye will see Him, even those who pierced Him, and all the tribes of the earth will mourn Him so it is to be. Amen." (Revelation 1:7 NKJV).

Elvera Young graduated from Bryn Mawr College with a major in English Literature and a minor in Women's & Interdisciplinary Studies. She has spent the bulk of her career in the field of Human Services and currently works for the Commonwealth of Pennsylvania's Department of Human Services.

Elvera was born, raised, and lives in Philadelphia, PA with her husband, children, and pet cats.

Seeking the Promises of God's Rest

We live in a world that is rapidly changing at an epic pace but not always for the best. For the past few years, we have lived with the traumas of over 6 million Covid-19 deaths, an unprecedented increase in global social injustices and unrest, senseless mass murders, occurrences of bizarre natural disasters, wars and rumors of war, and a rapid decline in moral values that threaten the core of our society.

When God promises, it forms a legally binding covenant that will never be broken. Whatever He says, we can count on Him doing it; that is when we ask in faith, not doubting, and believe we have it.

We live in a time of crisis—intense difficulty, trouble, or danger —and great stress. The daily vivid images shown on TV and other media continue to be a reminder of just how stressful things are.

When the global pandemic started in late 2019, like so many others, during the first years, I missed interacting with family and friends at annual family reunions, wedding celebrations, baby showers, holiday dinners, and church gatherings.

There were many nights of tossing and turning only to awaken the following morning with the bed covers on the floor, thinking about what was happening worldwide and if things would ever get better. Not only was I challenged with current societal issues, I was faced with my own personal crisis.

In February, I went in for what I had expected to be a routine yearly mammogram. The visit, to my surprise, was nothing at all routine. The imaging spotted a suspicious area that doctors wanted to investigate further by ultrasound.

After the ultrasound, the doctors recommended a biopsy to investigate the mass in more detail. The results were determined to be inconclusive, meaning the test was neither negative nor positive, making it impossible for a firm conclusion. The doctor recommended surgery to remove the mass for further evaluation. The surgeon discussed the findings and recommended an excision to remove 65% of the mass. According to medical statistics, my chances were 80% benign and 20% malignant.

I was not idle but continued to pray, study the Word, do personal ministry, and attend a church where we were blessed to hear messages of faith and prayer each week.

We are products of what we hear. If faith comes by hearing (Romans 10:17) and faith is the substance of things hoped for and the evidence of things not seen (Hebrews 11:1), it stands to reason that fear comes from what we hear and can influence whether we receive or resist the truth of God's promises.

After a few days, the surgery findings confirmed the mass was benign. Hallelujah!! Jehovah Rapha, the God that heals! Praise God for His fulfilled promise to be my Healer.

I was thankful for what the Lord was doing, but I felt that there was more He wanted me to learn, and I didn't want to miss it. According to Proverbs 25:2 (KJV), "It is the glory of God to conceal a thing, but the honor of kings to search out a matter."

So, I started searching the Scriptures for guidance. I was led to Matthew 11:28-29 (KJV), "Come unto me, all ye that labor and are heavy laden, and I will give you rest. Take my yoke upon you and learn of me; for I am meek and lowly in heart." There were several that stood out, revealing what God wanted me to see to embrace the process of receiving the fulfilled promises of His rest...

The word "come" is from the Hebrew word *Shaveta*, meaning return to the Lord. Deuteronomy 30:2-3 (KJV) says, "When thou shalt return unto the Lord thy God, and shall obey His voice according to all that I command thee this day, thou and thy children, with all thine heart, and with all thy soul; that then the Lord will return and gather thee from all nations, whither the Lord thy God hath scattered thee."

The Scripture "come to me" took me back to 1985 when I answered the invitation to come to Jesus and accept Him as my personal Lord and Savior. I recall when I had all the desired material possessions, a house, cars, and money in the bank, but lacked contentment and a sense of spiritual fulfillment.

The precious Holy Spirit has become my guide, protector, and comforter. My relationship with him has given me every right and privilege as an heir of God and joint-heir of Jesus Christ (Romans 8:17 KJV).

There will always be tests, trials, or tribulations that create stress in our lives. Amid the tests, trials, and tribulations, His desire is for us to live a Psalms 23 confession: "The Lord is my Shepherd, I shall not want."

The Lord calls us to come closer and learn of Him. We return to Him in our obedience to His voice. It is during this intimate time we spend with Him that He shows us His nature. In this place with Him, we can understand the magnitude of His love. He desires our complete surrender, confidence, attention, and trust.

We grow and are transformed into obedience to Him. Our obedience causes us to destroy the urge to war against the truth of His

Word and His promises. We are being transformed daily. He doesn't expect us to be perfect and do everything right, but He expects us to surrender and submit to becoming more like Him.

We can trust Him and let go the burdens of this world, believing in the nature of God, as Numbers 23:19 (NLT) says, "God is not a man, so he does not lie. He stands behind what He says, and his mind never wavers. Has He ever spoken and failed to act? Has He ever promised and not carried it out?" No, He hasn't, and He never will. Psalms 33:4 (NIV) "For the word of the Lord is right and true; he is faithful in all he does."

God allows trials and testing not to cause us to faint or grow weary but to come into the riches of our spiritual inheritance in Christ Jesus. He wants us to see His goodness while we are alive.

Now, I understand better that it isn't the blessing that gives me rest. It's the Blesser. It's not only the Word of God. It's the God of the Word. It's Jesus the Living Word. It's not just the healing. It's the Healer. It's not just about the deliverance. It's the Deliverer. Jesus wants to be exalted. He said, "And I, when I am lifted up from the earth, will draw all people to myself."(John 12:32 NIV).

God has given me promises that allow me to rest in faith and believe that I have them. Amazingly, I had an experience that would change my life forever for the better. I would like to share with you what happened... On the morning of January 6, 2023—my birthday— I awoke around 7:45am to a familiar voice that I recognized to be God's voice. While He was speaking to me, His voice wasn't forceful or loud but gentle, soft, peaceful, and full of compassion and love.

The conversation was very profound, yet so unexpected.–I wondered why today? I thought perhaps He had tried to speak to me on other occasions, but I was too busy to hear, or maybe I had ignored it. Possibly it happened because I was getting older and felt too tired to get out of bed. Now, He had my full attention.

Had the Lord decided to give me an extra special birthday present of an epiphany? I really can't say...but I am grateful that He spoke to me so precisely.... Well, by now, you are probably wondering, so what did you hear Him say? He said, "You are your greatest hindrance!" Wow! Say what?

When I am dealing with a crisis and don't draw near to and trust the Lord, "I am my greatest hindrance." I must always come to Him with my burdens, desire to learn more about Him, and cease trying to find my own solutions by obeying him. Essentially, this means I've accepted His love, joy, peace and the full finished work of the Cross. It is finished. (John 19:30 NKJV)

What a blessing it is to realize I can cease and desist from working in my own strength trying to please God, and instead see Him as the Promise Keeper. What a comfort it is to know my life is in His hands and whatever I am facing, moment by moment, He is with me, loves me, and will never leave or forsake me. He alone can settle all that is going on.

I've left the "Martha mentality" (Luke10:38 KJV), busy working on my own activities while neglecting the best part of sitting at His feet to learn, trust and rest.

I choose to obey His invitation to come, casting all of my cares on Him for He cares for me. (I Peter 5:7 CSB) I choose to be engulfed and comforted by His love—hearing the secrets that are only shared with me, His beloved!

We must all come to a place when we examine our lives and answer the question, "Will we be made whole?" Indeed it is time to stop allowing circumstances to hinder us and admit, we've been our own greatest hindrance by not believing we already have the promises of peace and rest from God.

My passion for loving God has grown. I will continue to develop spiritually through studying His Word, prayer, obedience, and fellowship with other believers.

I press toward the prize for which God has called me to know Him, to worship and submit to his lordship. Above all, to trust His promises. He is the One who knows me yet loves me, desires to spend time with me, is jealous for me, and doesn't want me to share the love and devotion that is His with anyone or anything else. He loves me with an everlasting love that doesn't waver, never fails, and forever calls me unto Himself.

He gave up His life so that I would enjoy everlasting life and all His promises, including His promise of *rest*. There is no need to stay awake to wonder, worry, or be dismayed about the world or personal affairs.

I already have access to every single one of God's promises, and I refuse to allow anything to separate me from the love of Christ Jesus and those promises. When spiritual rest is accomplished, physical rest is inevitable.

I am thankful to God for His Holy Spirit, who guides me in all truth and finding the promise of God's rest, and challenge you to embrace Matthew 11:28-29 (KJV) to come and find the promise of God's rest!

As I pondered writing a story for this anthology, the Holy Spirit; encouraged me with these words.

"You can't give up. I've called you to write in this season to convey My heart in written words to others. I will speak to you what you are to pen to others."

Wanda Nixon Brooks is an accomplished and seasoned Professional Certified Life Coach, with Solutions as Life Transforms, LLC. She is also Program Consultant, a workshop/seminar presenter, trainer, inspirational speaker, and minister. She is committed to helping individuals explore relevant solutions for their personal spiritual development and kingdom assignments.

God, Beauty, and Grace

I couldn't stay. The weight and burden felt too heavy.

My husband died at home, and home was where I was. His funeral had been only a few short days ago, the one-week anniversary of his death was approaching, and my emotions were too raw.

I fought to avoid re-creating the scenario of his death in my mind. My closest earthly relationship shattered and disrupted my life in ways that had been unimaginable weeks earlier as I sat by my husband's bedside during his last days.

I remember thinking, *I will be all right if I can get away, change the setting and my surroundings, and spend quiet time with God.*

Making a quick decision, I gathered the children together, and told them my plan. We packed our suitcases, and along with my sister who had flown out from Denver to be with me, we took off for the mountains of Virginia to a resort we had visited long ago as a 'whole' family. It was late at night when we arrived at our destination. Grief-worn and exhausted, we all went straight to bed.

Morning came far too early, and I rose with it. Grief washed over me immediately upon waking. Before my first thought was complete or even formed in my mind, I remembered... *He's gone.*

I slipped out of bed as quietly as possible to avoid awakening the kids or my sister who'd traveled from Colorado to join us. I put on what one of my friends describes as soft clothes, then walked out of the door and onto the deck.

I looked around the dusky backyard trimmed with leafy hedges and blossoming summer bushes.

Father, I am far from home, and it doesn't hurt any less.

I observed nature's backdrop, tree-lined vistas, deep azure mountain ridges, and a purple dawn sky. The sun was still in early calisthenic mode, with a few bits of light here and there but not yet ready for the full chin up over the earth's rim. *How,* I wondered, *was it possible to be in so much pain amid such magnificence and grandeur? Shouldn't one cancel out the other?*

Surely the God who paid such close attention to the details of creating a beautiful world and environment for mankind was equally— no, far more interested—in creating beauty in our heart.

Just a week earlier, there were kisses, listening to music, and prayers with my husband. Although he wasn't able to respond near the end or communicate, I was still his wife. As the days progressed and the disease begin to take more control of his body, I shared my heart with him and reminisced about the things we'd done together, our accomplishments and goals.

I felt the conflict between the two worlds—one world rejoiced at a homecoming; the other in deep bereavement at a death.

I wish I could say many Scriptures flooded my mind. Loneliness and pain prevented me from praying more than just a few words at a time. I'd found myself struggling to speak to God, to hear from God. It was hard to put into words the depth of my grief and how it affected me. I felt numb, blank. Yet, I knew I must trust the Lord, even through this storm.

The cool mountain breeze blew over my face, and I shivered. The slight chill I felt was in my heart, not the air. Warm tears ran down my face. I wondered again about being his wife and the words of the sacred vow "till death do us part." I thought of the countless applications I'd filled out over the past twenty years without giving much thought to the marital status boxes: single, married, divorced, widowed. *Was I still a Mrs.? Did I want to know the answer?* Never had I felt so fearful or alone. Life without my husband felt like being forced to walk on one leg.

Oh Lord my God, you who promised to never leave nor forsake me, why do I feel the opposite of those words? Why the feelings of complete isolation and desperate loneliness? How will I serve you, how will I walk through this time, without the love of my life? How will we make it as a family? I'm now a single mom. How do I find a way to give you glory, despite the anguish of my soul? How do I sing it is well when it is not?

I leaned forward, my head in my hands. Tears spilled from my eyes, splashed and splattered to the wood floor of the deck like rainfall. Tears of anguish and fear.

Caring for a husband who for six years was both paraplegic and suffering from dementia had caused me to grapple with the many challenges of being a single parent long before I officially became one. Tough decisions, home, auto repairs, managing the budget, child discipline and rewards, the rigors of home education. I juggled it all but never with the thought of eventual or complete control.

Being on the fringe of the single-parent lifestyle and the difficulties and challenges had been enough of a reality check to instill fear of what it would be like. Not so much fear of the unknown but fear of the known. I didn't want it and continued to weep.

Then I saw the deer. A mother doe and twin fawns, nibbling leaves and grass quietly, as I wept—quietly. It's amazing, as I think about it, that they noticed me about the same time I saw them. We both startled. Incredibly, the deer didn't bolt, and I didn't breathe.

The mother stared at me for a moment, and I stared back. I dabbed at my eyes and sniffled and watched.

She didn't take her eyes off me but continued to move agilely among the bushes. Eventually, she seemed to forget about my presence. They returned to their foraging, taking the occasional peek at me.

Watching the mother deer and her fawns roam through the wooded yard with such tranquility made a striking picture of beauty and grace. For the mother deer, seeking and finding all she needed for her family was her sole purpose in that hour. She went from tree to bush to grass, skillfully guiding her fawns with confidence. The fear in her eyes when she first spotted me soon left, and oddly, the doe did not appear to be afraid for herself or her fawns.

She'd been looking for food, and now she'd found it. The meal they needed most was the one they were having. Soon, all three deer stood within ten feet of where I sat. They grazed and stopped, grazed and stopped, and after a fifteen-minute interlude near my deck, they finally walked away. I watched until I could no longer see them. What a powerful lesson I learned that morning. The sweet voice of the Holy Spirit whispered, "She's a single mother, and if I have provided for her and her fawns, how much more will I do for you and your family, my daughter?" It was not by coincidence or imagination that light began to fill the sky as the sun peeked over the distant hills.

Watching the doe and her fawns, I was again reassured that the loving hands of the Father would always provide all I need, no matter how difficult the times or challenging the future. If I leaned on Him completely, trusted in His ability to meet my every need, I would be sustained by His provision and nurtured by His love.

I loved being the wife of someone who had loved me deeply and cared for his family fully. Our time together had passed. The tough days ahead were in God's hands. Only this truth kept me from becoming emotionally handcuffed. The enemy offers us shackles, but God's promises offer us freedom!

Since our escape to the resort in Virginia, there have been many difficult days. I cannot control the suggestions of dark thoughts that come as a result of grief. I can, however, control whether or not I breathe life into the suggestions. I alone control what I'll allow to consume me or exchange any dark thoughts with words of adoration and praise.

Although there may be times when my eyes strain to see the slightest ray of light, I do not need the bright glare of sunshine to assure me of daybreak or to know that the promise of joy will soon come. "Weeping may endure for a night but joy comes in the morning," Psalms 30:5b NKJV).

I've wondered about joy. *Joy.* We have a promise from our God that we are able to experience limitless joy in His presence and a deep fulfilling joy in life. Trouble is, there is a night time—rather many night times—of life through which we all must pass in order to find the reward of that special joy. I knew I had to reach deep in my heart for faith to believe I would survive the seemingly endless dark nights after such a loss.

Last spring, I saw three deer, a mother doe, and twin fawns drinking from the lake behind my house. I raced to grab my phone and take a picture. The last time I'd witnessed a doe and her fawns, the scene came with a promise, and here I was fifteen years later, looking at a magnificent reminder of God's long ago promise to me. My children, now adults, were always well provided for, as am I to this very day.

God has abundantly supplied every need, blessed many of my wants, and given me heart desires only He ever knew about.

I waited for, trusted in, and believed His promise. Looking at the deer from my deck reminded me of yet another promise He has fulfilled: "You have turned my mourning into joyful dancing. You have taken away my clothes of mourning and clothed me with joy" (Psalm 30:11, NLT).

Mari Fitz-Wynn is a nonfiction author, novelist, poet, and songwriter. She is a much sought-after speaker whose talents have carried her across the globe. Her works include *Take Heart: 26 Steps to a Healthy Home School, Connect the D.O.T.S.*, and most recently, her debut poetry collection *RISE UP! Poems of Protest, Poems of Praise* is her third book to be published. In 2018, she received a prestigious United Arts Professional Development Literary Grant for her upcoming novel, *Deep Secrets, Deeper Faith* (2023). She was honored in April 2022 during National Poetry Month with one of her poems selected to appear in the *ExperieNCe Poetry! 30 days of poems by 30 N.C. writer*s.

Mari has written numerous articles for various women's magazines and her state's home education magazine. She has written litanies and poems for years, several appearing through *Engage Worship* in the U.K.

An editor and writing coach with twenty-five years of experience. She is passionate about helping writers of varying experiences and started a writer's group in 2016, *The Answer is Write*. Becoming an author caught Mari by surprise. Twenty-five years ago, she penned her first story. Today, she is still passionate about capturing in words, stories, and poetry about people she meets and places she visits.

In her limited free time, Mari enjoys reading, spending time with her adult children, teaching and training others for pursuing prayer and healing ministry, and finding clever ways to train her seemingly untrainable dog, Ducky.

Bible Translation Abbreviations

AMP - The Amplified Bible

CEV - Contemporary English Version

CSB - Christian Standard Bible

ESV - English Standard Version

HSCB - Holman Standard Christian Bible

KJV - King James Version

MSG - The Message

NASB - New American Standard Bible

NIV - New International Version

NKJV - New King James Version

NLT - New Living Translation

TLB - Living Bible